Eric Sloane

RECOLLECTIONS *in Black and White*

Recollections

IN BLACK and WHITE by ERIC SLOANE

 WALKER AND COMPANY · NEW YORK

First published in the United States of America in 1974 by the Walker Publishing Company, Inc.

Published simultaneously in Canada by Fitzhenry & Whiteside, Limited, Toronto.

ISBN: 0-8027-0461-1

Library of Congress Catalog Card Number: 73-90383

Printed in the United States of America.

10 9 8 7 6 5 4 3 2 1

Dedicated to those who enjoy taking ink from an ink-well and distributing it beautifully and wisely upon white paper; to those who think with their hand and an uninhibited pen; and to those of that golden age of illustration who inspired me to recollect the American scene in black and white.

STATEMENT

The simplest and most intellectual of the arts is the black line on a white background; no other medium can better recall the diorama of memory than simple line drawing.

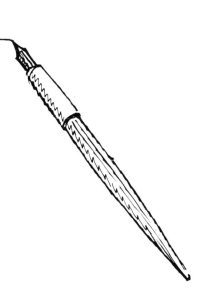

Winter

There are few better places to observe the outside world than from an attic window. Framed by the inside darkness, the eye of an old house looks out over the scene aloof, detached from the seasons and the constant business of daily life below. The quiet on that certain day was broken only by the soft hiss of hail blowing across the roof. The landscape was blanketed, making it difficult to believe that any life could have existed beneath the snow. It was a proper time and place for reminiscing.

Old attics seem to be havens of forgotten memories and like man's own uppermost storeroom (his brain) they are places where all sorts of things are stored awaiting rediscovery and the eventual process of recollection. It was while packing away some Christmas tree decorations that I happened across one particular memory from the morning of my days, a battered portfolio of writings and pen and ink drawings which I had done over half a century ago. The portfolio was marked MANUSCRIPT FOR SHAPES IN BLACK AND WHITE, and I was startled at recognizing

8

my own lettering and furthermore to realize that my handwriting could have changed so little over the years. Even the pen and ink sketches might have been done yesterday; only the paper had aged.

It was just the sort of thing that I needed on that cold and wintry day. Christmas holidays had always left me in a melancholy mood and I had been morbidly comparing nature's annual seasons with the seasons of man's own life, thinking also how my personal season of winter appeared to be spending itself in a final and all too uninspired chapter. The old manuscript was a fresh and reassuring tonic, still alive with the invigorating springtime of my early self.

As I scanned the material, I realized that our thoughts are ageless and that a worthwhile plan is never completely obsolete, its reason-for-being always returning at some time or other with the cycle of time. My manuscript had actually become more pertinent now than it could have been fifty years ago.

I have always said tongue-in-cheek that the easiest way to learn any subject at all is to write a book about it, and this old portfolio contained my very first effort to prove that outlandish and brazen theory. It was an arrogant principle but it was compelling enough to have plagued me throughout the years and finally to result in some three dozen books on various subjects. So it seems to have worked for me.

It all began once upon a very long while ago when, starting my term at art school, I found my lessons disappointing and unrewarding and I decided that perhaps analyzing art itself and writing a paper on the subject of drawing might give me better results than my trying to learn anything from teachers. Presumptuous upstart that I must have been, there nevertheless was worthwhile thought in my unusual theory that primarily, art deals in *shapes* rather than *outlines,* and therefore the very first thing an art student should do is to learn to see the world about him only in *shapes,* forgetting outlines.

It must have exasperated my professors for I refused to use my stick of charcoal in the orthodox manner (like a pencil) to outline drawings with its point. Instead, I laid the stick flat upon the paper and scrubbed in large masses of shadow and created major shapes of light: details and outlines were added almost reluctantly afterward. I considered art a reflection of life itself; and in life, after all, overall observation, planning and purpose should come first while details should be considered later. An inspired revolutionist was I.

My schooling was obviously short-lived so I left my studies to set about trying to see the world in shapes. A portrait study, or a still life or landscape scene held no promise at all for me unless it was first an interesting composition of *shapes.* A barn, for example, might be completely unsuitable to paint at midday (casting little or no shadow), but in the early morning or in the late afternoon when it was transformed into a composition of triangles of shadow and rectangles of light instead of just an outlined barn, that same structure became an exciting and irresistible subject. Corot said, "In the early morning or late evening one can see nothing but everything is there. At noon, one can see everything but nothing is there." I was convinced that the student who learned to ignore outlines and see everything in shapes would at once become an artist even before he tried his hand at drawing. Art school, with its outlining first and adding shading later of vases and plaster casts and skinny men in jockstraps, was not for me. Leonardo da Vinci said, "The boundary of bodies is the least of all things. O painter, do not surround your bodies with lines!"

My manuscript on this subject never did reach the publishing stage but the album of pen and ink illustrations, which were involved, led me off into a lifetime adventure in black and white that has ever since been my constant enjoyment.

Among the ink sketches that I found in the attic was a long-forgotten Christmas card from "Everard." This was done just before the time I had left home to find for myself in a newly found world as a sign painter, when I had decided to begin anew, starting from scratch with a different name. I then had changed my actual name Everard to Eric: Hinrichs (my last name) became Sloane. The old Christmas card revived distant memories for it featured a black sheep (*that* indeed was Everard!) who evidently thought that the holy season was the proper time for a black sheep to come out of hiding long enough for a polite greeting to his family and friends. I suppose I was eccentric even then (and I am thankful for that) because the plain white paper was trimmed with a wide black ribbon which made it look more like a death notice than a Christmas card. This must have baffled those who received it and would have been rich in meaning to any psychoanalyst. "Another year," it read. "Greetings, Everard, 1923."

I also found a faded advertisement from *The New York Times,* which I immediately recalled because it had resulted in the only salaried job that I have ever had. "Wanted, a good black and white artist to start at twenty-five dollars a week."

You don't hear much about "black and white artists" nowadays because commercial art is so dominated by color art and color photography; but back when twenty-five dollars a week was an acceptable salary, most illustrations were monochromatic. Graphic studios had little equipment other than white paper, black ink, white showcard paint and the pens and brushes to apply it with.

ANOTHER YEAR GREETINGS! EVERARD 1923.

the difference between *Seeing in outline . . . and*

Seeing in shapes.

Details are Afterthoughts.

Although art schools tend to teach outline first and consider shadowing of secondary importance, the composition of shadow shapes as shown here is of primary importance. Animals that see in black and white and gradations of gray, recognize things by shape: you may dress differently without your dog noticing, but move in an odd manner or change your shape in some way and he will become startled at once. But man is so accustomed to regarding details and dress, that seeing in shape has become a neglected art.

First snow

the Composition of
Shadow shapes

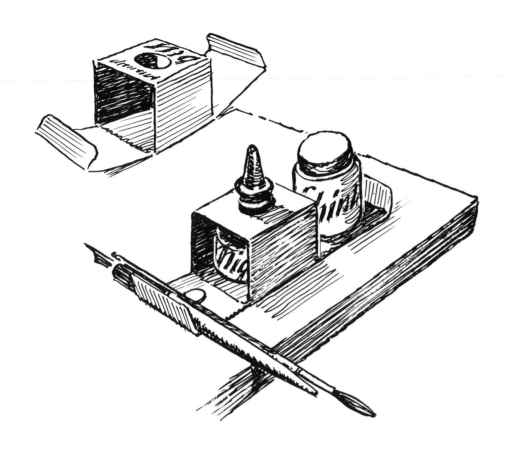

The father of my first love, the girl next door, had inspired me to become an artist for he was one of the more successful black and white illustrators of that time. He did pictures for *Field and Stream* magazine, but his greater income came from doing pen and ink catalog illustrations for Butterick Patterns. I remember his robust ladies posed in long underwear and children in shorts, shirtwaists and panty waists. A page full of those drawings took him less than a day to do but they made for him as much money as the average man earned in a whole month. When other daddies had their breakfasts and were well on their way to work, Herman Rountree in his plus-four knickers and tweed cap, was out walking with his pipe and his dog before the day's work. That, I decided, was not work at all; it was a beautiful way of life, and so a good pen and ink artist I'd become. The artist delights himself to the extent of wanting nothing else in life but the privilege of expressing himself, so I am forever thankful for my decision. Now that I look back, I guess I was less in love with the girl next door than I was admiring of her father, for he was my secret hero.

Generally speaking, the day of the hero belongs to the past. Today is an age when apprenticeship is looked upon as condescending, old-fashioned and according to present union ethics, against the law. Following in the footsteps of another, when I was a boy,

was the wise and proper thing to do and the world was delightfully rich with all sorts of heroes. There were people to admire in politics, favorite writers, inspiring actors and artists whose techniques were worth practicing. Artist Herman Rountree's Butterick Patterns were not so inspiring to me but his *Field and Stream* covers and animal drawings certainly were, and my first decision was to become a nature artist. I recall collecting a file of his published work (art students called that a "morgue") hoping to acquire his technique at nature art. But alas my abilities were not most suited to animal drawing; I remember having such difficulty with drawing horses' legs that I usually compromised by having my animals standing in high grass. Twenty-five dollars a week for doing lettering and simple commercial art seemed a better way for me to start, and I answered that ad.

My first job, however, did not last very long but I do remember being impressed by the vast amounts of black ink and white paint being used at that time and wondering if instead of drawing, I should not go into *that* business. Ink had always fascinated me; it seemed to have a wonderful aura of decision, finality and permanence. As a child I had experimented with ink-making, trying early American methods with squeezed walnut hulls, indigo juice, madder, fruit acids and charred potato skins (or lamp soot) to produce a black. The manufacture of ink was already an interesting challenge, so either brave or stupid or simply young, I contacted manufacturing chemists and soon mixed what seemed to be a good waterproof black ink. Then I arranged to buy white showcard paint wholesale, so that I might be in both the black and white manufacturing business. I designed cartons and registered the name "Nig" (for my black ink) and "Chink" (for my Chinese white). Those made two great trade names then, but obviously would not be very popular now.

My adventure into commerce, however, was short; I learned that the businessman and artist are two entirely different people. "Nig" and "Chink" never reached the public market and I was left with a thousand printed cartons and my first batch of waterproof black ink which I stored in a dozen cases of discarded Moxie bottles. When I first set out in the family's Ford roadster as a mobile sign shop, my supply of black ink was much more than adequate; the rattling of Moxie bottles heralded my arrival wherever I went, even louder than the old Model-T engine.

I was not the first artist to start as a lowly sign painter. Many of the early American painters began by doing tavern signs; furthermore it seemed to be a great way for a young fellow to see the country. The old-timers, of course, went by foot or on horseback and

by comparison, in my Model-T, I traveled in grand style. A canvas awning which stretched from the auto top to the ground made a fine tent at night and, although it was before the invention of the rumble seat, there was still room in back for everything a young artist could want for his studio. If it had not been for my great supply of black ink, I might have specialized in pencil-sketching. But being frugal had its compensation, for to this day I still seem to think in black and white, in pen and ink.

The idea of sketching the countryside, as I sign painted my way across the United States, was inspired by a twin-volume set given to me by my father, called *Picturesque America.* Done in pen and ink and steel engraving, Hudson River school artists had therein compiled a portfolio of drawings that dramatized the American scene; their presentations were so different and startling that most of my boyhood nightmares were enacted from pages of that book. There was something dramatic and haunting about them.

The trick, it seems, was not to draw a landscape as one might see it from the comfort of any conventional viewpoint; instead, the artist climbed to a dizzy position aloft and looked down upon the scene. Then to add to the tenseness he would put tiny figures in a precarious position, ready to slip and fall into space. A balanced rock scene would be enhanced by the fig-

those dramatic landscapes from
"Picturesque America"

ure of a man sleeping peacefully and unconcerned under it; a simple town panorama would be viewed from the very top of a church spire; no cliff was complete without a couple of people standing inches from doom and one felt an immediate urge to shout out and warn them to stand back. This trick of the Hudson River school of art made each landscape an unforgetta-

ble experience. Besides inspiring me to do black and white sketches of the American scene, I am sure it also influenced my interpretation of the dramatic in both thinking and writing. I still have those two volumes and I still find enjoyment and fascination in its unusual presentations.

ERIC SLOANE, SIGNPAINTER 1925

It was not until my traveling studio was packed and underway that I realized my license plates (long expired) had been removed. But my ability to letter came to the rescue; the lid of a shoebox made a presentable and convincing license plate and I painted my family's telephone number thereon and proceeded westward (legally, I presumed) into my career of itinerant sign painter.

When a commercial sign was needed on the plain cement wall of a building, I thought I was cheating by using some of my black ink; but whereas a proper black paint would have weathered and peeled off in time, my "Nig" sank into the porous cement and if those walls still remain I am sure that my signs are there too. The lasting power of ink is remarkable—whereas many of the finished works of the old masters have since cracked or faded, some of their preliminary ink sketches are still as fresh and clear as the day they were done.

Lancaster
County

My first stop of any length was near Lancaster, Pennsylvania, where I thought I might settle long enough to use much of my ink supply. (The people there seemed to have a fanatic aversion to color and a religious reverence for black.) Clothing, signs, automobiles, carriages and whatever might have been colorful were instead rendered black by the Amish people. Painting over chromium was almost a business in itself, but my sign work and lettering on mailboxes was most remunerative.

My knowledge of German Black Letter (which we often incorrectly refer to now as "Old English") gave me an instant entrée to the Plain People of the German area who enjoyed "Fraktur-writing." This decorative calligraphy harkens back to the time when vital statistics were preserved by law in Germany; all family records such as births, deaths, marriages, land deals or even important celebrations were recorded by trained scriveners, made decorative and suitable for framing. The lettering was usually more fancy than legible with Spencerian embellishments of distlefinks, cats, dogs, tulips and only God knows what else. "Herr Everard Hinrichs der Fraktur-schrifter" did many a Fraktur in his homemade black ink that has since shown up in antique shops as pure Americana. (Eric Sloane is sorry about that.)

Everard Hinrichs

signs and lettering

19 25

You can't blame a young fellow for trying to be a good businessman. An announcement card which I tacked on a bulletin board of a Lancaster restaurant, this was probably the last time I used my real name of Everard Hinrichs. Otto Heinrich was a well-known Lancaster County decorator of the late 1700s, whose Fraktur *work was still revered; so as Herr Hinrichs I felt at home plying my sign and lettering trade among the Plain People.*

Lancaster
Pennsylvania

Pennsylvania German

My short stay with the Amish was an experience worth recollecting, for I found myself living much as the early American would have done in the 1700s. The early Amish were farmers who had come to America to escape military service because, being God-fearing, they objected to hate, murder and therefore warfare. They still refused to insure their lives or property for that would be betting on death and destruction, which would show a lack of complete faith in God. They also refused to participate in social security; their answer to the problem of making a living was simply *hard work*. Family security and neighborly help took care of both the aged, the sick and the needy. Now, half a century later, I still find myself presenting the Amish argument, writing the gospel of their religion and painting the scenes of their Americana. I still salute them as extraordinary Americans with a philosophy (now more than ever) worthy of recognition. With their farms and windmills and horses they are the least touched by an energy crisis: their only crises are the surrounding developments of an exploding population that threaten their contentment and way of life.

My introduction to barn lore began in the Lancaster area; the pen sketches I did there resulted in a reverence for old farm buildings and the wish to learn more about them. But there wasn't a single volume written about the subject and so I resorted to my "learning by writing" theory by doing a first book about the early American barn. Later when I started *An Age of Barns* (1963) I retrieved several drawings

Pennsylvania
Barn hood

from my first sketching tour when I had gone from farm to farm selling drawings of the farmers' barns. The Amish were not prone to hanging pictures on their walls, but the fact that I worked in black ink seemed to make some difference. My price for a barn portrait was only five dollars but that was standard weekly salary for a live-in farmhand so I was faring very well indeed.

I recall having done several barn decorations, usually involving the name or initials of the owner; but the true Pennsylvania German barn was either plain or whitewashed and void of any decoration whatsoever. I cannot recall any reference to "hex signs" and I am convinced that this idea evolved recently: fifty years ago I found the Plain People without superstition and strict in their religion against decoration. Probably the first attempts at barn decoration started when gable and brickwork was introduced and ventilating windows were designed as openings in the shapes of diamonds, tulips, hearts, crosses and even men on horseback or attempts at initials and dates. I suppose the encouragement of this inventive flair started the timid designs on barn door hoods and finally evolved into designs across the whole face of the barn known as "fancy Dutch."

Of course there was no superstition involved such as "scaring away evil spirits" as legend has it and the farmer simply decorated his barn in pride, just as his wife decorated her patchwork quilts with the same star-shaped designs. However, the old-school Amish criticized their "fancy neighbors" and in sheer ridicule called their outlandish barn decorations "hexe schrift" (witch writing). The tourists and press were delighted and the name "hex sign" has stuck ever since.

I remember one farmer who was proud of his very large cow and insisted I do a painting of it on his barn. Deciding to be quaint, I tried to do an American "primitive" with exaggerated body and tiny legs. It ended such efforts from that day on for a farmhand looked on in wonder and said, "Good Gawd, what a hawg!"

My supply of "Nig" was being used, but not having invested in manufacturing "Chink," I had to do without the white paint. I must explain that white was often used partly like an eraser to clean up pen drawings and also to soften whatever ink lines were too heavy. So being without white paint, I scratched away my mistakes and softened too-heavy lines with a razor blade, inventing an idea which has been a part of my technique all these years. I now buy my razor blades in lots of a thousand and whereas I might shave twice with the same blade, I usually use a new blade for each sketch. I am glad that I didn't have white paint with me on that first sketching trip.

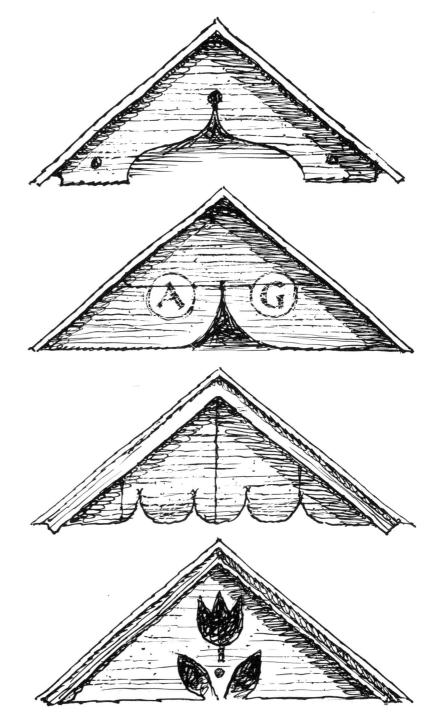

Another trick with white was "spatterwork," the showcard painter's delight, making a pattern of mist or snow by combing through a toothbrush filled with either ink or paint. As corny and commercial as it seems now, spatterwork was accepted as an illustration technique.

White is not always blankness; it can portray vast-ness, coldness, loneliness, quiet, solidity or empty space, as the artist so wishes. Here the white paper of the page itself becomes the stillness and contours of snow-covered land. The eloquence of plain white can be exquisite.

Chester County

Once a toll house . . .
. . . Horseshoe Pike

36

Lancaster County

Much more an artist's subject than a practical home, this upright type of early Pennsylvania German stone house seems to have been built without plans. Rising from too little ground space, with windows placed at random as the building proceeded and with stairways more like ladders, comfort was confined only to the snug feeling of compactness and the consequent ease of heating during wintertime.

The European logic that a house, like a man's clothing, needs only to be big enough to fit himself, is evident in this architecture: many early Pennsylvania houses almost look like a man. The tall fellow at the left even has hips and shoulders. Few of these stone buildings are left now, although fifty years ago they were accepted Pennsylvania domestic architecture.

Pennsylvania was first in covered bridges from the start (and still is). In 1805 after the Great Permanent Bridge (over the Schuylkill in Philadelphia) had been built and was already in operation, artist Charles Willson Peale offered the idea of making it more permanent by building a roof over it, and so introduced the first covered bridge in America. I sketched nearly three hundred Pennsylvania bridges (more than there were in all of New England) and I still wonder why Vermont has always been known as America's "covered bridge state"; after Pennsylvania, Ohio, Indiana and Oregon, it ranks only fifth.

Hundreds of the old covered bridges have since been destroyed, some burned, others fallen into disuse and final decay, but the stone abutments which are still evident are probably the greatest examples of early American ruins. We are so involved with building anew and tearing down whatever even hints of age that we have too little reverence for the architectural past and no regard at all for ruins. We have few noble ruins left and have nothing but contempt for the dignity of pleasing decay: any architecture seems acceptable in our present-day world as long as it is *new*.

I still find the ruins of ancient barns or collapsed bridges irresistible to sketch, but I feel that I have failed when I am regarded as "one who makes pictures of ancient barns or collapsed bridges." What I believe I have been doing these past few years (or have tried to do), is depict and narrate the aura of a rich and historic past—the building itself in each picture is only the catalytic symbol to portray a certain mood, and not the subject.

The Amish had no reverence for money and found the greatest pleasure in exchange of goods or a "swap." Striking hands in closing a bargain was "mit swappen" akin to the Germanic schwappen *(to whack) and I painted many a sign "mit swappen." One mailbox sign and piece of* Fraktur *was done in exchange for the rare print (shown opposite) of America's first covered bridge. It shows traffic passing over before the sides and roof were decided upon; the tiny middle picture shows it finished.*

It seems that the builders were embarrassed about the cost of the bridge being more than the national debt at that time, and to make the bridge appear more lasting they added sides, coated it with cement paint and roofed it over, calling it "permanent." All other bridges followed suit and in 1805 the American covered bridge was born.

SCHUYLKILL BRIDGE High Street PHILADELPHIA.

The Bridge as it appears now covered

"Householder Bridge"

Southern Ohio Covered Bridges

These are two of nearly a hundred Ohio covered bridges from my original research album. For a while, Ohio had more covered bridges than Pennsylvania but over half of them were burned, many during the Civil War period. Ohio's bridges are unusual, some having flattish roofs and some having the wooden awnings shown in these two southern Ohio models. Both have since been destroyed.

Rainbow Bridge (1850)

The very first covered bridge I sketched was one over the Ellis River in Maine, resulting in my first covered bridge painting (now in the book and on the cover of I Remember America). I remember it because it sold in a gallery for $750 which seems very little nowadays; but the bridge itself cost less than that to build back in 1866. To be exact it cost $743.43, including stone abutments!

Ackley
Bridge

This is the way Pennsylvania's Ackley Bridge looked in 1925. By 1935 the truss had weakened and the bridge was doomed for removal. But it was eventually chosen for Henry Ford's Greenfield Village at Dearborn, Michigan, so it was lowered onto the ice of Enslow's Fork in 1937, dismantled and shipped for restoration. It stands there today, a typical example of the early Pennsylvania covered bridge, nearly a century and a half old, yet still in use.

Lancaster Country

RECOLLECTIONS IN

Allegheny cascade

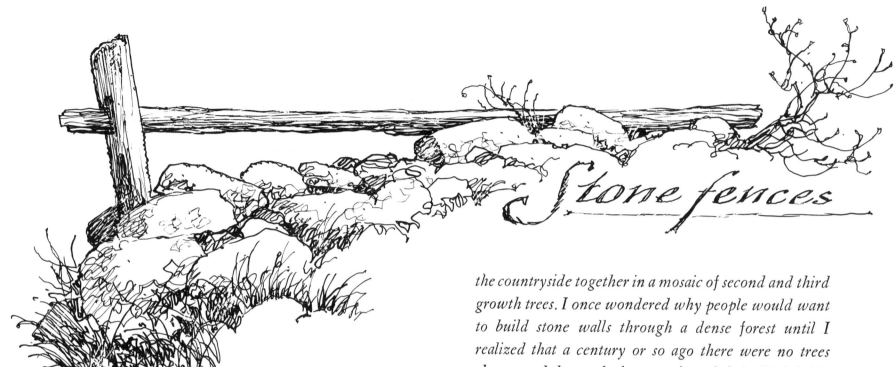

Stone fences

the countryside together in a mosaic of second and third growth trees. I once wondered why people would want to build stone walls through a dense forest until I realized that a century or so ago there were no trees there—and that as the farmers cleared their tilled fields, they just piled the stones in rows along boundary lines or pastures.

Now and then I have happened across zig-zag stone fences in the forest, wondering why anyone would build anything but a straight line fence. The answer to that one is that it first was a wooden snake rail zig-zag fence and the farmers simply piled stones up and against that. As the old snake rails rotted away and disappeared, a solid stone zig-zag fence remained. Another mystery was solved.

Looking almost like a wallpaper pattern, the sketch opposite was my observation from a hilltop.

With the first snow, New England's stone fences stand out like the stitches of a patchwork quilt, lacing

American
Ruin

Mesa
pueblo

RECOLLECTIONS IN

Nature never lets up ~ ~ ~ ~ ~ ~ to see man's buildings in her own image ~

into the prairie (at some risk) to meet and visit with one of the wagon travelers. When I was met with a leveled rifle, I felt like someone in the cast of a western movie, and when the old fellow shot into the ground a few feet from me, I decided it wasn't make-believe. I suppose there were still those who simply preferred the old ways.

It was natural that I found my way south to the Vieux Carré of New Orleans which was a magnet of Old World decadence in a beautiful and constant state of siesta. Fifty years ago when I set up a springtime studio on St. Peters Street near Royal, there were few houses equipped with electricity; there were old people in the Latin Quarter who had not yet been to modern Canal Street only a few blocks away. Voodoo was practiced openly and there were occasional sex circuses in the streets. Recently I visited these haunts to find the buildings unchanged but taken over by a Coney Island mood with modern topless and bottomless cafes and "adult exhibition" performances on Royal Street. I suppose the Latin Quarter has not changed spiritually much more than it has architecturally. Pleasing natural decay and moral decadence are so often the unique aesthetics of a Bohemia.

Everyone who visits the old quarter of New Orleans feels that he has discovered it. Degas "discovered" it in 1872 and wrote to artists James Tissot and Henri Rouart: "Fair France still has a quarter of a foot in Louisiana . . . everything is beautiful here in this world of people . . . Manet would see lively things here—even more than I do."

A new theater had opened when I first arrived in New Orleans and I managed to get the job of lettering the lobby signs and doing the marquee banners. I remember that the main attraction was the invention of a man named Hammond who had created a massive electric organ which, as it played, started from the bottom of the stage pit and rose pneumatically to an elevated position high in the center of the stage.

My sign work was usually finished by midnight and I hung it during the dawn so I suppose, being sleepy, I made occasional mistakes. When the manager phoned me one noon and dismissed me, I first presumed it was because I had used black ink instead of the color he insisted upon. But his displeasure involved my wording on the marquee banners. ONE OF THE WONDERS OF THE AGE, the signs said. COME EARLY AND WATCH HAMMOND'S ORGAN RISE. "Try to be funny somewhere else!" he thundered. I left the next day, sketching as I went, again painting signs for traveling expenses.

From New Orleans, my mobile sign shop headed west and soon reached another Bohemia of that day at Taos, New Mexico, where I settled long enough to

finish off my entire supply of black ink. I even sold some of it to the Indians and you can still find occasional Taos pottery decorated with my homemade ink.

I set up a little sign shop on the outskirts of Taos, at "Kiker's Cabin Camps" on the road to Cimmaron Canyon, where the Taos Indians frequently danced for the tourists. The dance leader named Juanito Luhan taught me dance steps and some of their songs well enough to become their impresario. I made posters and announcements, and we went as far as Raton and Pueblo, entertaining at fairs and theaters. But most of all I recall making a hoop for Juanito's young nephew; the Indians had never seen such a toy but little Bobby had ideas other than rolling it along with a stick—he began to *dance* with it. And that, believe it or not, was the origination of the well-known "ancient American Indian hoop dance." Now they use as many as six hoops in this dance.

The village of Taos was an artist's gathering place, started by the "original seven" painters (Bert Phillips. Ernest Blumenschein, Victor Higgins, E. Irving Couse, Joseph Sharp, Oscar Berninghaus and Walter Ufer). Phillips and Blumenschein had "discovered" the place when their covered wagon broke down there years before, and by the time I arrived it had become a national art center.

The Log bridge to Taos Pueblo 1925

With my base at Taos, my Model-T took me to deserted mining places, abandoned missions, ghost villages and the ruins of ancient New Mexican culture, an area which provided endless subjects for drawings. The black and white technique was perfect for depicting that blasting sunlight and devouring shadow so typical of the bright western landscape. Western artists who paint in color *on location* are frequently blinded by the intense sunlight, resulting in hazy pastel scenes that seemed bathed in mist, quite the opposite of the true western vision which is crystal clear and where even distant mountains loom distinct.

My pen and ink drawings sold quickly to tourists and provided me with money for the paints that wooed me away from monochrome and started me on a half-century of painting in color with oils. But I recall Leon Gaspard, whose paintings are now famous for their astounding brilliance, encouraging me to stay with my pen and ink. "Some day," he declared, "I shall paint with color and get the same impact as you do with the power of black and white." I am sure he was just being kind to a young fellow, for Gaspard, the king of color, had nothing to learn from any living artist or from any other medium than his own.

In those days when most printing was done in color, there were giants who spoke with just their pens. Howard Pyle, N. C. Wyeth, A. B. Frost, Frederic

WAGON TRAIN

Mission ruin.

Ranchos de Taos
Mission

Done as preliminary sketches for an oil painting, these two rough ink drawings on the Ranchos de Taos adobe mission of St. Francis of Assisi illustrate the value of shapes of light and shadow. Half closing your eyes, you can see as much or even more of the subject than with your eyes wide open; at least so is the effect.

This rear view of the old building has since become a popular subject for Taos artists, the coloring and planes of sunlight and shadow changing constantly. As seen from the highway, this "symphony in mud" has become more familiar than the more traditional front entrance which faces the hills, and except for an occasional plastering of fresh adobe mud, it remains quite as it was in 1718.

Remington; from the Hudson River school to the "ashcan school," American illustrators had amassed a remarkable heritage of excellence with nothing but black ink upon white paper. The well-chosen line had become the national shorthand of art. We might easily forget the authors of tales like *Alice in Wonderland* or *The Wizard of Oz* or *Uncle Remus,* but the illustrative characters by Tenniel and Denslow and Frost are indelible, quite as important as the written stories that they walked in.

Those golden days of pen art featured names that are now being revived as nostalgia, but the real truth is that their monochromatic art was just as powerful as that of color. Edward Penfield, Franklin Booth, Heinrich Kley, Joseph Pennell and Charles Dana Gibson are still American giants. *Collier's* magazine made one contract for Gibson's ink sketches for one hundred thousand dollars (something like a quarter of a million dollars in today's values).

The fact that each famous black and white illustrator had his own technique and that he was a social commentator of his time, made him both artist and historian, a person of national importance. Nowadays the pen and ink illustrator is not even recognized as a true artist. Color, whether sprinkled carefully in the manner of Jackson Pollock or vomited out blatantly on a canvas in de Kooning style, makes the colorful abstract modernist the favorite artist of our present day.

There are those whose fascination for color has blinded them to the value of black and white; but if this page were printed with each letter a different color, they would find it almost unreadable and realize how color is not always superior: the simple impact of communication would be gone, lost in an unbelievable confusion of color. Shakespeare who wrote, "Black is the badge of hell, the hue of dungeons and the scowl of night," should have known better, for his own words have been kept alive with good black ink.

The colored painting is usually designed to deceive the eye. The black and white picture which cannot deceive the eye in any way, is intended only to stimulate the mind of the beholder and communicate a pictorial message. The very monochrome words you are now reading are exaggerated examples of this truth.

I confess to having been influenced by the hypnotics of color and I have even regarded my own original drawings with so little value that I often gave them away to whoever bought the first few copies of the book they illustrated at a book autographing party. It is sad that the worth of art is estimated more in money than in spiritual values. But wrongs do have their compensations, for it was when I saw some of those early gift illustrations auctioned off at what my oil paintings brought that I was startled into a proper regard for pen and ink, and the importance of black and white.

I suppose if people finally become jaded by color photography and the modern art circus of "pop" color, we might witness a renaissance of the monochrome sketch and experience a return to pen and ink art. We have regarded pen drawing as being limiting to self-expression, yet it is the most demanding and revealing test of the artist's ability, in no way mimicking nature or the camera as a painting does. Realism (usually more craftsmanship than art) must be accomplished only with paint. A pen and ink drawing can never be possibly mistaken for a camera picture; it is as genuinely an expression of the artist as his personal writing.

Comparing a pen and ink drawing to letter writing is not farfetched for (like his writing) each pen sketch is completely the maker's own work. It is actually more difficult to copy than anything he can do with paints and brush. (I find it easier to imitate an artist's work than to forge his signature.) A black and white pen drawing is actually a personal statement in the unique "handwriting" of the artist.

The artist's sketch is usually something done quickly but at a studied speed. Often the quickest line best captures the artist's impressions. Your casually written signature is a unique expression, completely yours and nearly impossible to forge, yet if you were asked to take one or two full minutes to make that same name, the result would not be recognizable (even to you) as your signature. That same casual, studied speed applies also to the artist's sketch. The first quick sketch of a major work in oils is often a more personal and a better form of art than the final tedious finished work in color where the artist has painted out his free thought with the craftsmanship of paint.

Lucky is the artist whose quick sketch and finished work are both the same thing. Those like Heinrich Kley who used his pen "like the lariat of a temperamental cowboy" captured thoughts as quickly as they entered his mind. Only a very few have mastered the art of intelligent doodling, sketching in a casual manner without planning and encouraging design to flow like a beautiful involuntary exercise conceived by an inborn source. Some painters accomplish this effect immersed in background music while they work. I, too, find that helpful.

I used to have my telephone attached to a remarkably equipped easel and as some people doodle with a pencil on a pad while at the phone, I painted. Not every telephone call was engaging and most of them were lengthy so I found a fair amount of time to paint in a free and detached manner and without much thought. Several of my more acceptable works happened to be these "telephone paintings" which began